NIAGARA FALLS

ROYAL
SPECIALTY
SALES

DISTRIBUTED BY

Royal Specialty Sales
Toronto, Canada
Tel. 416-423-1133 Fax 416-423-0991

INDEX

© Copyright 2000 by EditProjet, Paris

Photos on pages 3-5, 8-12, 13 bottom, 14, 15, 16 bottom, 17, 18 top, left and right, 19-21, 22 bottom,
28, 29 top and bottom right, 30 centre and bottom, 31, 32, 34-37, 42, 43, 44 top and bottom, 46-51, 54-59, 62,
courtesy of Royal Specialty Sales.

Photos on pages 24-25 and 52-53 - courtesy of New York State Office of Parks and Recreation and Historic Preservation.
Photos on pages 26-27 - courtesy of Winter Festival of Lights.
Photos on page 38 - courtesy of Skylon Tower.
Photos on pages 39 left, top and bottom, 40 - courtesy of Niagara Falls Museum.
Photos on page 45 - courtesy of IMAX Theatre.
Photos on pages 60-61 - courtesy of Inniskillin Wines.
Photos on pages 62-63 top and middle right - courtesy of Niagara-on-the-Lake Chamber of Commerce.
Photos on pages 63 bottom, 64 - courtesy of Fort Erie Economic Development Corporation.

The publisher is thankful to the NPC for its cooperation.

Printed in Italy by C.S.E.B. Sesto Fiorentino (Florence) - Italy

#862561
ISBN 2-84339-023-0

* * *

A 19th-century illustration of the Niagara River, just downstream from the Falls.

Niagara Falls, one of the world's most spectacular natural wonders, is known for its breath-taking beauty and for the host of attractions that make this area a great vacation destination. The Falls today are also a marvel of hydroelectric engineering, and they are fixed in popular imaginations as a Mecca for honeymooners and death-defying daredevils.

In 1678 a missionary traveling with the explorer LaSalle, Father Louis Hennepin, recorded the first eyewitness account of Niagara Falls. From colonial times through the War of 1812 the British and French, and then the British and Americans, jousted for control of the Niagara River and the strategic 9-mile portage around the Falls.

Tourists began to arrive here after the War of 1812; in 1827 the first stunt was performed to attract the tourist trade. A junk schooner, the Michigan, was loaded with animals and sent over the Falls.

Daredevils have been ingeniously challenging the mighty Niagara for well over a century. The earliest stunts were those of tight rope walkers, the most famous being The Great Blondin in 1859 and 1860. Not only did Blondin walk across the Niagara Gorge on a tight rope, he also crossed blindfolded, riding a bicycle, walking on stilts, pushing a wheel-barrow and carrying his manager on his back. Others soon followed, including Maria Spelterina who crossed in 1876 with baskets tied to her feet.

The first person to successfully challenge the cataracts was Annie Taylor in her 1901 barrel trip over the Horseshoe Falls. The school teacher's oak barrel was padded with pillows and had an anvil in its bottom to ensure that it floated downriver in an upright position. Since that time, many stunters have attempted to defy the Falls in various barrel like contraptions, including William Red Hill Jr.'s "The Thing", which was made of thirteen inflated inner tubes tied together with canvas webbing and fish nets, and Nathan Boya's rubber covered steel ball. Not all the daredevils were as fortunate as Annie Taylor and many have lost their lives in their attempts to challenge Niagara.

Unplanned fame came to 7-year-old Roger Woodward, who in 1960 was swept over the Horseshoe Falls unharmed, after a boating accident on the Upper River. More recently, on September 26, 1993, Canadian Dave Mundy became the only person to survive two barrel rides over the Falls. (Thrill-seekers note: Niagara Falls stunts are now discouraged by fines up to $10,000.)

3

BOBBY LEACH and his Barrel after his perilous trip over Niagara Falls, July 25th, 1911.
(Copyright 1911, U.S.A. & CANADA by Bobby Leach.)

Top left: Annie Taylor was the first to "barrel" over the Falls and live to tell about it.

Top right: The Great Blondin carrying his manager over Niagara River.

Bottom left: Bobby Leach spent years on the lecture circuit after surviving a trip over the Falls in a steel barrel.

Top: An 18th-century engraving of Niagara Falls by J.P. Cockburn.

Bottom right: Canadian Dave Mundy is the only person to make two trips over the Falls.

Pages 8-9: A panoramic view of beautiful Niagara Falls, from the Canadian side.

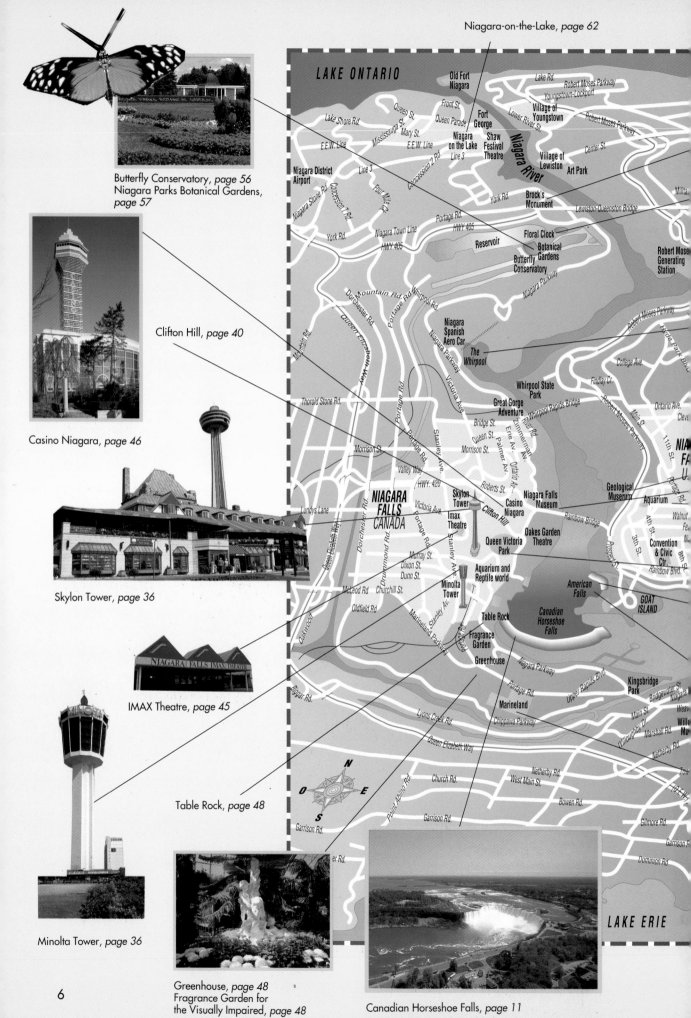

LAKE ONTARIO

Old Fort Niagara
Lake Rd.
Robert Moses Parkway
Youngstown-Lockport
Front St.
Fort George
Village of Youngstown
Lower River St.
Robert Moses Parkway
Queen St.
Queen Parade
Lake Shore Rd.
Mississauga St.
Mary St.
Niagara on the Lake
Line 3
Shaw Festival Theatre
Center St.
E.E.W. Line
E.E.W. Line
Village of Lewiston
Niagara District Airport
Line 3
Concession 2 Rd.
Art Park
York Rd.
Brock's Monument
Lewiston-Queenston Bridge
Niagara Stone Rd.
Concession 7 Rd.
Four Mile Cr.
Portage Rd.
HWY 405
Milita
York Rd.
Niagara Town Line
HWY 405
Reservoir
Floral Clock
Robert Moses Generating Station
Botanical Gardens Conservatory
Mountain Rd.
Dorchester Rd.
Portage Rd.
Whirlpool Rd.
Niagara Parkway
Robert Moses Parkway
Niagara Spanish Aero Car
Hyde Park Blvd.
Niagara Parkway
The Whirlpool
College Ave.
Queen Elizabeth Way
Whirlpool State Park
Findlay Cr.
Ontario Ave.
Cleve
McArthur Rd.
Great Gorge Adventure
Whirlpool Rapids Bridge
River Rd.
Robert Moses Parkway
Main St.
11th St.
NIA
FA
U.
Thorold Stone Rd.
Portage Rd.
Victoria Ave.
Bridge St.
Zimmerman
Queen St.
Erie Av.
Ontario Av.
Palmer Av.
4th St.
Geological Museum
Aquarium
Morrison St.
Stanley Ave.
Morrison St.
Roberts St.
Niagara Falls Museum
3rd St.
Walnut
Fe
Valley Way
HWY 420
Skylon Tower
Casino Niagara
Rainbow Bridge
NIAGARA FALLS CANADA
Victoria Ave.
Imax Theatre
Clifton Hill
Prospect St.
Convention & Civic Ctr.
Lundys Lane
Dorchester Rd.
Drummond Rd.
Portage Rd.
Stanley Ave.
Queen Victoria Park
Oakes Garden Theatre
Rainbow Blvd.
Murray St.
Dixon St.
Dunn St.
Aquarium and Reptile world
American Falls
GOAT ISLAND
McLeod Rd.
Churchill St.
Minolta Tower
Oakwood
Oldfield Rd.
Marineland Stanley Pkwy.
Stanley Av.
Fragrance Garden
Canadian Horseshoe Falls
Kingsbridge Park
Table Rock
Bigger Rd.
Greenhouse
Niagara Parkway
Portage Rd.
Upper Rapids Blvd.
Bridgewater St.
Niagara
Wea
Main St.
Will
Mu
Lyons Creek Rd.
Marineland
Willoughby Dr.
Marshall Rd.
Chippawa Parkway
Netherby Rd.
Queen Elizabeth Way
Tot
Church Rd.
Netherby Rd.
West Main St.
E.E.W. L
er Rd.
Point Abino Rd.
Garrison Rd.
Bowen Rd.
Gilmore Rd.
Garrison F
Garrison Rd.
Dominion Rd
LAKE ERIE

N
O
E
S

Floral Clock, *page 58*

Brock's Monument, *page 58*

Niagara Spanish Aero Car, *page 55*
Niagara Gorge, Whirlpool Rapids, *page 55*

Geological Museum, *page 52*

Niagara Falls Museum, *page 42*

Aquarium of Niagara Falls, *page 52*

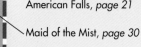

American Falls, *page 21*

Maid of the Mist, *page 30*

Queen Victoria Park & Oakes Garden,
page 44

Marineland, *page 50*

Fort Erie, *page 64*

CANADIAN HORSESHOE FALLS

Seen from the ground or from above, by day or by night (when powerful colored spotlights illuminate the Falls in a rainbow of hues), the Horseshoe or Canadian Falls is an unforgettably magnificent sight.
The Horseshoe Falls are 170 feet tall (comparable to a 16-story building) and 2,600 feet long. The Maid of the Mist pool beneath the Canadian Falls is 180 feet deep - dug ten feet deeper than the river bed by the persistent stream of pounding water. There are a number of taller waterfalls around the world, but the huge amount of water flowing over Niagara Falls makes it the greatest waterfall on earth, when judged by volume.
Flowing just 35 miles from Lake Erie to Lake Ontario, the Niagara is a dramatic, if abbreviated, river. It splits into two channels around Grand Island, New York, and flows along at a languid five or six miles per hour until reaching the Upper Rapids three miles above the Falls. Here, at the Point of No Return, the river's pace accelerates to upwards of 42 miles per hour. After rushing over the

Falls, the Niagara River flows through narrow, turbulent Niagara Gorge and the Whirlpool Rapids, past several picturesque towns and restored forts into Lake Ontario.
A popular way to experience the Horseshoe Falls is at ground level, via the Journey Behind the Falls, located in Table Rock House Plaza. Twin elevators descend to a 150-foot tunnel leading to viewing portals behind Horseshoe Falls and a roaring, drenching outdoor observation deck at its base. (Raincoats are provided - you'll need one.) Back up top, enjoy lunch and a commanding view of the Falls at Table Rock Restaurant.
Niagara Falls are illuminated for approximately three hours every night of the year by phalanx of colored spotlights. The Falls were first lit in 1860 for Britain's Prince of Wales, on the eve of the Great Blondin's sensational tightrope walk across the Upper Great Gorge of the Niagara River. In the 1870s, each lamp provided 2,000 candlepower; today a single Xenon gas torch produces 250 million candlepower. On Friday nights in the sum-

Left, top and bottom: Rainbows and mist over the Canadian Falls.

Below: An aerial view of the Falls and Canada's Skylon Tower.

Above and right: Ninety percent of Niagara Falls' flow goes over the Canadian Falls.

Left, top and bottom: As many as 12 million tourists annually come to Niagara Falls; many visit these popular observation points on the Canadian side.

Following pages: An aerial view of the Horseshoe Falls.

mer and on major Canadian and American holidays, brilliant fireworks displays light up the sky above the Falls.

Early on, Niagara was a popular destination for European royalty. The area won its abiding reputation as the "Honeymoon Capital of the World" in 1803 when Napoleon Bonaparte's brother, Jerome, married a woman from Baltimore, Maryland, and visited Niagara Falls on his honeymoon. (Unfortunately, this union was annulled two years later.) Since that time, the area has catered to newlyweds, who still visit annually by the thousands.

The name "Niagara" is thought by many to be derived from "Onguiaahra," an Indian word believed to mean "Thunder of Water." A more likely, if mundane, translation is "strait" or "throatway," referring to the portage around the Falls cleared by Indians. In any event, primitive and modern men alike have marveled at the fearsome din of the Falls. "The true voice of Niagara," wrote 19th-century American author Nathaniel Hawthorne, "is a dull, muffled thunder, resounding between the cliffs." In 1683, Father Hennepin wrote that the Falls "thunder continually, and when the wind blows in a southerly direction, the noise they make is heard ... for more than fifteen leagues." (Niagara Falls, in fact, has impressed many authors, such as Charles Dickens, who wrote: "Niagara was at once stamped on my heart, an Image of Beauty.") In geologic terms, the 12,000-year-old Niagara Falls are a relatively new phenomenon. About 20,000 years ago, water from a melting glacier created the Niagara River, which flows across a 500-million-year-old shelf of rock known as the Niagara Escarpment. Over the years, the

These pages: Close-up views of the rim of Horseshoe Falls.

These pages: More birds-eye shots of the Horseshoe Falls, plus colourful night views of both Falls.

Below: As illustrated here, the rate at which Niagara Falls is receding has considerably slowed.

river has eroded the escarpment. This erosion has caused its hard dolomite and limestone top layer to collapse in places on to the soft shale and sandstone layer underneath, thus creating the Falls (this has occurred twice, actually) and pushing them upstream. Just since 1764, the Horseshoe Falls has receded 865 feet towards Lake Erie. Until the 1950's, erosion caused the Falls to recede three feet per year, but thanks to remedial works and the power projects — less water flow, less cutting power — that rate has dropped to less than one foot per year, perhaps as little as one foot per decade.

The first electric generator on the Niagara River began operating in 1893. Today the Niagara Power Project is one of the world's major hydroelectric operations. Among the largest plants here are the Canadian Sir Adam Beck Niagara Generating Stations and the Robert Moses Niagara Power Plant, on the American side.

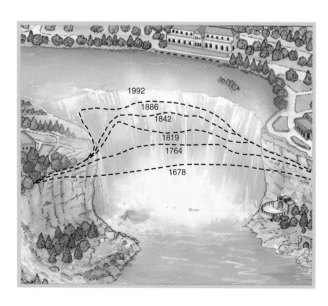

Left: The two cascades of the American Falls, including the delicate Bridal Veil Falls.

Above: The American Falls with the Horseshoe Falls to the right.

AMERICAN FALLS

The American Falls are actually two falls separated by Luna Island - the major cataract and a smaller cascade, the delicate Bridal Veil Falls. The larger of the two is sometimes called Rainbow Falls, named for the rainbows that continuously form in the mist above Niagara Falls.

The American and Canadian Falls are separated by Goat Island, part of the United States. Local lore has it that long ago a goat was the lone survivor of a particularly harsh winter on this island, hence its name. Others say Goat Island is named for goats once stored here by Indians.

Goat Island is today part of 400-acre Niagara Reservation State Park. Established in 1885 by then-governor (later president) Grover Cleveland, it is the oldest state park in America. Getting around the reservation is easy;

The Viewmobile constantly makes the rounds, transporting tourists to six stops at scenic points. The New York State Park Visitors' Center here offers information exhibits and the Niagara Festival Theater, which shows the giant-screen 3-D thrill film, "Niagara Wonders."

The park also includes Prospect Point, Terrapin Point and the New York State Park Observation Tower, a 282-foot-tall glass, aluminum and steel structure rising 100 feet above the American Falls. From the top of the New York State Park Tower sightseers enjoy a spectacular overview of Niagara Falls, while two glass-walled elevators descend to the base of the gorge. Here you can board the Maid of the Mist for a memorable, if soggy, boat tour of the turbulent Niagara Falls basin.

The Cave of the Winds guided trip begins at the base of the Bridal Veil Falls, accessible via elevator. The visitor is

provided with protective rain gear as part of the tour. One hikes along a wooden walkway to the aptly-named Hurricane Deck and along catwalks behind the Falls leading to Goat Island.

The Niagara River pours over the American Falls from a height of 184 feet, somewhat higher than the Canadian Falls. The American Falls are 1,060 feet long and handle just 10 percent of the total flow of the Falls. Over the years boulders and rock debris called talus have accumulated at the base of the American Falls, reducing the water's fall by almost a third. Talus continues to build here, and in 1969 water was temporarily diverted from the American Falls by the U.S. Army Corps of Engineers in order to study this phenomenon. It was decided that nature should be allowed to take its course, for fear that removing the talus could collapse the cliff wall. Consequently, debris now rises two-thirds up from the base in places. At this rate, the American Falls may become steep rapids in less than 100 years.

Top left: Visitors at the Cave of the Winds.

Below: The American Falls, from the Canadian side.

Right: An observation platform at Prospect Point overlooking the American Falls.

Top left: The American Falls with New York State Park Tower and the Rainbow Bridge in the background.

Below left: Indian statue at Prospect Point.

Top and middle right: The American Falls.

Below right: The Viewmobile transports sightseers along the American side of Niagara Falls.

FESTIVAL OF LIGHTS

The Festival of Lights takes place annually, usually from mid-November to mid-January. Parks on both sides of the river are transformed into a wonderland of animated lights, fireworks and historical tableaux. Observation towers and other attractions glitter, while concerts and holiday programs celebrate the season.

These pages: Millions of electric lights and fireworks illuminate the annual Festival of Lights.

Following pages: For several hours every night of the year, colored spotlights paint Niagara Falls in a rainbow of hues.

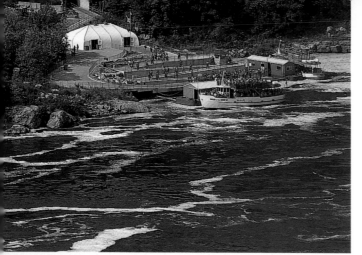

MAID OF THE MIST

One of the most spectacular views of the Falls is from the deck of the Maid of the Mist boat. In operation since 1846, thousands of rain gear clad visitors make the trip each year. Cruising past the base of the thundering American Falls, the boats propel their way upstream into the basin of the turbulent waters below the Horseshoe Falls. While the original Maid of the Mist was a wooden-hulled sidewheeler, powered by steam from a coal fired boiler, the current four boats are steel hulled and diesel powered. On at least one occasion, in 1960, the Maid of the Mist served as a rescue vessel, fishing young Roger Woodward out of the Niagara Falls basin after his amazing impromptu dog-paddle over the Canadian Falls.

The Maid of the Mist is named for the heroine of a local Indian legend. Long ago, tribe members who lived along the river began to die of a mysterious sickness. As a remedy, it was decided that the maiden Lelawala be sacri-

These pages: The Maid of the Mist propels tourists to a close-up and thunderous view of the Falls.

These pages: Protected by rain gear, tourists can view Niagara Falls from the Maid of the Mist.

ficed to the thunder god, Hinum, who lived with his sons in caves behind the falls. She went over the roaring water to her death and, while falling, was caught in the arms of Hinum's sons. They told her that a giant water snake was periodically poisoning village water. Her spirit alerted her people, who mortally wounded the snake on his next deadly foray. As he fled back to the river, the snake twisted into the semi-circular shape that became Horseshoe Falls.

From approximately early May to late October (depending on the ice) the Maid of the Mist departs every 15 minutes from either the Canadian or American side of the river. Passengers are provided with rain gear for protection from the spray.

WINTER IN NIAGARA FALLS

Freezing weather transforms Niagara Falls into an enchanting fairyland. Winters are bitter cold here and it's not unusual for ice on the river to accumulate to a thickness of 50 feet. Mist and spray from the Falls freeze on lampposts, fences and trees creating spectacular protean shapes, illuminated at night in dazzling colors.

Ice from Lake Erie is often blown by winter winds into the river's mouth. In 1938, ice on the river up to 80 feet thick crushed the 40-year-old "Honeymoon Bridge." Winter conditions can also create an ice bridge, in times past the site of toboggans and souvenir vendors. Old photographs show ladies in long skirts and gentlemen in top hats strolling across the ice bridge. Such activity was banned in 1912, after three people, including a honeymoon couple died when a section of the ice bridge broke off and floated downstream.

These pages: Dazzling natural ice sculptures form around the Falls each winter.

Above: The Skylon Tower is the tallest tower above Niagara Falls.

Below: The Incline Railroad and People Mover are popular ways to get around the Canadian side of Niagara Falls.

SKYLON & MINOLTA TOWERS

The 775-foot Skylon Tower offers soaring panoramic views of Niagara Falls and the surrounding area. This popular Canadian landmark features a three-level dome with indoor/outdoor observation decks and two revolving restaurants. At the base are shops, an arcade and exhibits. Fast external elevators ("Yellow Bugs") zip to the top of Skylon Tower in just 52 seconds.

Also on the Canadian side, the Minolta Tower rises 325 feet above Horseshoe Falls, with eight floors at its top surrounded by glass specially designed to facilitate photography. There's a Minolta exhibit floor, comedy club, the Pinnacle Restaurant and state-of-the-art video simulator rides. The dazzling Waltzing Waters light, sound and water show is presented here nightly May through October.

This page: Various views of the Skylon Tower and one of its restaurants.

This page: The Minolta Tower offers a sweeping view of the Niagara region.

39

CLIFTON HILL

There's a carnival atmosphere along Clifton Hill in Niagara Falls, Canada. A short walk from the Horseshoe Falls, this neon-lit strip of amusements, museums, fun houses, restaurants, beer gardens, motels, shops and kiddie rides annually entertains millions.

Museums are a big draw. Ripley's Believe It or Not! Museum, a favorite on Clifton Hill, showcases the unique and bizarre. Nearby, The Guiness World of Records recreates some of the world's most amazing feats.

The Movieland Wax Museum features life-like images of film and television stars. Louis Tussaud's Waxworks displays history's most famous figures; a more infamous group can be found in his Chamber of Horrors. A similar display of dubious human endeavor can be found in the Criminals Hall of Fame Wax Museum around the corner on Victoria Avenue.

These pages: The bright lights of Clifton Hill signal fun, family-oriented attractions.

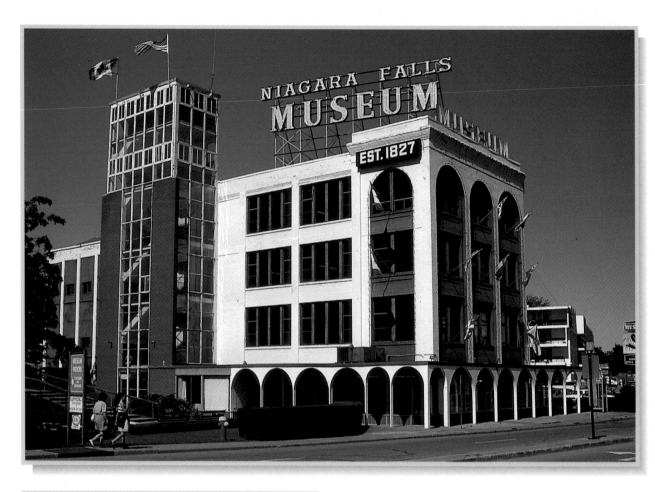

NIAGARA FALLS MUSEUM

As one might expect, the Niagara Falls Museum specializes in local history. It is a happy surprise, however, to find here artifacts from around the world, including a remarkable collection of Egyptian mummies.

A life-size reproduction of a triceratops dinosaur, typically covered with climbing children, guards the entrance to this facility. Inside are 26 galleries containing more than 700,000 artifacts. The "Daredevil Hall of Fame" features a figure of Annie Taylor in her barrel, plus a display of other contrivances sent over the Falls.

There's also a "Hall of Dinosaurs," "Rock and Mineral Collection" and an exhibit on "Niagara's Power and Industry." Military enthusiasts will enjoy "Ancient Guns and Weapons" and "Oriental Curios," featuring a life-like Japanese warrior in full regalia. See a Canadian Indian burial ground located in "Indian Lore," then explore the amazing "Freaks of Nature" collection of oddities such as a stuffed two-headed calf. A humpback whale skeleton dominates the "Geological Collection."

By far, the jewel in the crown here is the "Egyptian Collection," with some of the world's oldest, best-preserved mummies. A 1994 episode of National Geographic Explorer, "Mr. Mummy," features this exhibit, and can be seen in the museum's new mini theater.

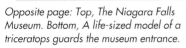

Opposite page: Top, The Niagara Falls Museum. Bottom, A life-sized model of a triceratops guards the museum entrance.

This page: Right, top and middle, Niagara Falls Museum exhibits include daredevil memorabilia and prehistoric skeletons. Left and bottom right, The Niagara Falls Museum's notable Egyptian collection includes the mummy of General Ossipumphenoferu.

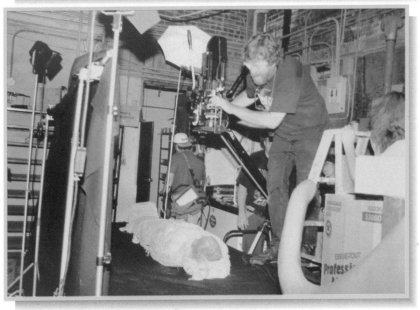

This page: Views of Oakes Garden.

QUEEN VICTORIA PARK & OAKES GARDEN

Queen Victoria Park, established in 1887, stretches along the Canadian side of the Niagara River adjacent to the Falls. Canada's first provincial park, it offers acres of beautifully-maintained formal gardens, walkways and many spectacular views of both cataracts — especially the Horseshoe Falls. Every spring the park is blanketed with more than a half-million brightly-colored daffodils.

The delightful Oakes Garden is located next to Queen Victoria Park at the foot of Clifton Hill, on the site of the old Clifton Hill Hotel. Formally opened in 1937, the Oakes Garden Theatre features a Greco-Roman amphitheatre, with the stage situated so that the Falls form a dramatic backdrop to any production. Two open-air pavilions, European-style gardens and lily ponds adjoin the amphitheatre and provide a gorgeous venue for leisurely relaxation.

IMAX THEATRE

What Niagara Falls vacation would be complete without the traditional trip over the Falls in a barrel? These days, fortunately, one can experience virtually all the excitement and terror of such derring-do in the plush, harmless comfort of a modern cinema at the IMAX Theatre - Canada's largest movie screen.

For daredevil wannabes, "Niagara: Miracles, Myths and Magic" is the next best thing to your own stunt. Shown on a 6-story screen, this thrilling film is billed as the "most spectacular IMAX adventure of all."

Created by Academy Award®-winner Kieth Merrill, the film relates the epic history of Niagara Falls. Its focus includes early Indians, the War of 1812 and, of course, the daredevils.

While at the IMAX, visit Daredevil Adventure, the world's largest collection of daredevil artifacts and barrels. A video shot by Dave Mundy as he plunged over the Falls is continuously screened here. Newspaper clips, photos and recordings also tell the curious story of the Niagara daredevils.

Top: A scene from "Niagara: Miracles, Myths and Magic".

Bottom: The pyramid-shaped IMAX Theatre offers thrilling armchair trips over the Falls.

CASINO NIAGARA

I f Lady Luck ever rode shotgun on those barrel runs over the Falls, it's a good bet she can be found today at Casino Niagara, where modern-day daredevils take their chances at slot machines or gaming tables.

The gambling boom that swept North America has come to this area in a big way: Casino Niagara has 96,000 square feet of gaming space, 3,000 slot machines or video poker and 123 gaming tables. As you enter, marvel at the 3-story atrium waterfall.

Besides gambling, there is much food and shopping at Casino Niagara. Mediterranean cuisine is the fare at Farfalle (Italian for "butterfly"), named for the Niagara Parks Commission's Butterfly Conservatory. Entrees are prepared tableside at The Market, open 24 hours a day. Marilyn's penthouse lounge, one of seven bars here, features live entertainment. You can dispose of your winnings at any of eleven gift shops on the premises.

Located within walking distance of the Canadian Falls, Casino Niagara is open 24 hours a day, year-round.

Left top: Casino Niagara as seen from Oakes Garden.

Left middle and opposite page: The Casino Niagara tower rises above its 3-story atrium.

Below: Modern-day daredevils try their luck at Casino Niagara.

TABLE ROCK

The name "Table Rock" is derived from the 200 foot-wide shelf of rock that once jutted 60 feet out of the gorge overlooking Horseshoe Falls.

In 1850 this promontory collapsed into the churning waters with a crash that jolted inhabitants for miles around. The remains of Table Rock were blasted off in 1935.

GREENHOUSE

More than 400,000 visitors annually tour the Niagara Falls Greenhouse, south of Horseshoe Falls. Known for its colorful seasonal flowers, Greenhouse displays range from autumn mums to Easter lilies to Holiday poinsettia. Gloriously-colored tropical birds fly free in the Tropical House, which features exotic international flora. Twenty varieties of floribunda comprise the Rose Garden, located in front of the Greenhouse. The Butterfly Garden here cultivates flowers that entice local species of butterfly.

FRAGRANCE GARDEN FOR THE VISUALLY IMPAIRED

The Fragrance Garden, adjacent to the Niagara Greenhouse, is a sensual delight — specifically the senses of smell, taste and touch. Many of the more than 100 specimens of this horticultural attraction are chosen for their powerful, delightful aromas — an olfactory, as well as visual, feast. Hence, a number of plants here are labeled in Braille.

The Fragrance Garden is at its peak in June, July and August.

Bottom: The Fragrance Garden, next to the Greenhouse, is an olfactory delight.

Opposite page: The Greenhouse produces beautiful seasonal flowers, year-round.

MARINELAND

Located upstream from the Canadian Falls, Marineland is the area's most popular attracton after the Falls. Its thrilling Aqua Theatre Show stars acrobatic killer whales, vivacious dolphins and charming sea lions, while an aquarium showcases colorful undersea life. In the petting park, more than 500 friendly deer mingle with visitors. See also elk and buffalo, while playful bears roam Bear Country. Exciting thrill rides include one of the world's largest steel roller coasters, Dragon Mountain.

These pages: Talented animals and other attractions of Marineland.

AQUARIUM OF NIAGARA FALLS

Those of us without gills and fins will appreciate the arid comforts of the Aquarium of Niagara Falls, which promises visitors: "We've brought the ocean indoors for you." The more than 1,500 aquatic creatures in residence here seem content with the Aquarium's impressive amenities, as well.

The list of ocean-going inmates is substantial: performing dolphins, sea otters, moray eels and vivid tropical fish marked by a spectrum of colors. You'll be extra thankful for thick glass when a school of piranha or a toothy shark glide by. The Aquarium is also the perfect place to see the closer-to-home inhabitants of the Great Lakes. Here, too, is the Northeast's largest collection of fresh-water gamefish. Outside the main facility, sea lions disport themselves in an outdoor pool that's free of charge to onlookers. Also of particular interest: a colony of rare, endangered Peruvian penguins.

Located a short walk from the American Falls, the Aquarium of Niagara Falls is open year-round.

GEOLOGICAL MUSEUM

Anyone interested in geology will naturally be intrigued by Niagara Falls, a rock hound's dream vacation spot. Both serious and amateur geologists will enjoy exploring the Schoellkopf Geological Museum, located on the American side of the river, on the edge of turbulent Niagara Gorge.

This spiral-shaped facility houses extensive and fascinating exhibits on regional geological formations. The emphasis here is on the 435-million-year geologic developmental history of Niagara Falls and the relatively recent actual appearance and recession of the Falls over the last 12,000 years.

The Geological Museum tells this vast story using exhibits, interpretive programs and audiovisual presentations, including multi-screen slide shows. Weather permitting, there are guided walks through a rock garden and nature trail on the museum grounds, and to the scenic Niagara Gorge overlook.

The Schoellkopf Geological Museum is open daily from April to October. Off-season, the museum is open Wednesday through Sunday.

Above left: The Aquarium of Niagara Falls is home to more than 1,500 aquatic creatures.
Middle left: A view of Niagara Falls from the New York State Observation Tower.
Bottom left: A hiker in Whirlpool State Park.

Above right: The Geological Museum.
Bottom right: Old Fort Niagara overlooking Lake Ontario.

NIAGARA SPANISH AERO CAR

On the Canadian side, downstream from the Falls, the Niagara River passes through a narrow gorge and the turbulent 60-acre Whirlpool basin. Boating here is roughly equivalent to barrelling — that is: really, really dangerous. A more sensible way to observe the Whirlpool Basin is via the Spanish Aero Car, built in 1916 by Spanish engineers. Supported by modernized 1,800-foot cables, the Aero Car offers a thrilling, no-risk, birds-eye view of the swirling waters.

NIAGARA GORGE

The Niagara River travels downstream from the Falls through a narrow pass between steep heights. This gorge is 11 km (7 miles) long and extends from the Falls. Within this stretch of turbulent waters lies the treacherous Whirlpool Rapids, so named because of the giant Whirlpool formed at their base. The rapids stretch for 1.6 km (1 mile) and are best viewed from the canyon floor at the Great Gorge Trip. Visitors can access the lower gorge by way of an elevator that descends through a 70 m (230 ft) shaft and adjoining 73 m (240 ft) tunnel. Once at the rapids edge, the visitor can view the awesome spectacle by wandering along the adjacent scenic boardwalk.

Left and right, top and bottom: The Spanish Aero Car crossing the turbulent Niagara Falls Whirlpool basin.

Right middle: Whitewater enthusiasts will not want to miss the Great Gorge Adventure.

WHIRLPOOL REVERSAL PHENOMENON

The Whirlpool Rapids flow into the 120-foot deep Whirlpool, located at a 90 degree bend in the river three miles below the Falls. At the Whirlpool you can witness the Reversal Phenomenon, where water from the rapids enters the pool, then travels counterclockwise.

When the water tries to cut across itself to get out, pressure builds that forces the water under the incoming stream, creating a vortex.

Reversal of flow

Normal flow

BUTTERFLY CONSERVATORY

"Flowers in flight" are the enchanting main event at the Niagara Parks Butterfly Conservatory, located in the Niagara Parks Botanical Gardens. Around 2,000 butterflies reside here, representing approximately 50 species.

This climate-controlled 11,000 square-foot facility provides a perfect environment for butterflies and the flowers that are their food sources. A hatching area is set aside for butterflies emerging from cocoons.

After first-hand study along a 60-foot network of paths, visitors also learn about these fascinating creatures at an on-site auditorium and two theaters.

Above: The Butterfly Conservatory provides for an amazing nature study.

Below: A typical tenant of the Niagara Falls Butterfly Conservatory.

*This page: The immaculate Niagara Parks Commission
Botanical Gardens and the Butterfly Conservatory are
maintained by ambitious School of Horticulture students.*

NIAGARA PARKS
BOTANICAL GARDENS

The Ice Age returns annually to the Niagara region, which may account for the passion for flowers and gardens that's so evident here during the temperate months. A case in point: the Niagara Parks Botanical Gardens and School of Horticulture. Canada's only residential school for apprentice gardeners, this is where many talented amateurs go to turn pro.

The Botanical Gardens and School of Horticulture are located six miles above the Falls on the Niagara Parkway. Every year a half-million visitors stroll through this lovely immaculate 100-acre campus, established in 1936. From herb and vegetable plots to an enormous elaborate rose garden, many outstanding examples of the gardener's art are produced here by hard-working students; their ambition and competitive spirit are reflected in the excellent quality of the landscape.

An arboretum at the Botanical Gardens features several hundred trees, including a first-rate collection of ornamental varieties. Horticulture students also tend the new nearby Butterfly Conservatory.

Above: Niagara Falls' Floral Clock is among the largest such attractions in the world.

Opposite page: Imposing Brock's Monument honors a Canadian hero of the War of 1812.

FLORAL CLOCK

Farther along the River Road north of the Botanical Gardens is the Floral Clock, built in 1950. Modeled after a similar clock in Edinburgh, Scotland, the Floral Clock is designed using 15,000 plants and changed twice a season. With a forty-foot diameter, it's among the world's largest such attractions.

BROCK'S MONUMENT

The massive ornate memorial to Sir Isaac Brock dominates Queenston Heights Park, scene of an early and decisive battle in the War of 1812. Canada's first military hero, General Brock was killed by a Yankee sharpshooter in the Battle of Queenston Heights, but not before he rallied British troops to fend off the American invaders. Some historians indeed believe that the U.S. might have successfully conquered Canada during this conflict, were it not for Brock's leadership and tactical skills.

General Brock and his aide-de-camp, Captain John Macdonell, are entombed in a vault in the 185-foot-tall monument. A narrow winding staircase inside leads to an observation deck offering a commanding view of the Niagara River and environs.

A walking tour of the Battle of Queenston Heights begins at Brock's Monument. Other park attractions include a picnic area, tennis courts, a bandshell, kiddie wading pool, restaurant and snack bar.

NIAGARA WINERIES

If not for the Falls, the Niagara region might well be best known today for its wineries. If the area seems too far north for this to be true, remember that Canada's Niagara Peninsula is located on the 43rd latitude, the same as northern California and actually south of Burgundy, France.

This is a cold-climate viniculture region, like Burgundy, Oregon, Germany and New Zealand. Primarily due to low harvest temperatures, such regions produce typically lighter and fruitier wines, such as Chardonnay, Pinot Noir and Riesling.

One of the Niagara region's premiere wineries, Inniskillin Wines, Inc., is headquartered on an old Niagara-on-the-Lake estate. A re-

These pages: Scenes from Niagara's wine region. Left, above and below: Locally-grown fruits for sale, plus grapes on the vine awaiting harvest.

stored barn houses Inniskillen's tour centre, the starting point for a fascinating first-hand inspection of the winemaking process.

About two-thirds of Ontario's fruit orchards are in Niagara, accounting for most of the province's peaches, cherries, pears, plums, prunes and grapes. Roadside produce stands and "pick your own" farms provide visitors with an opportunity to experience the best and the freshest of the harvest.

Above left: Wine aficienados enjoy the products of the wine-makers' art.

Above right and middle: Inside a Niagara winery.

Bottom right: An array of Niagara wines.

Above: Charming Niagara-on-the-Lake is one of the most picturesque towns in North America.

NIAGARA-ON-THE-LAKE

Lovely Niagara-on-the-Lake, located on Lake Ontario at the mouth of the Niagara River, has carefully preserved its Old World appearance and sensibilities. There's a pronounced lack of neon in this quiet, picturesque village — in striking contrast to the roar and bright lights of Niagara Falls, just 13-and-a-half miles south.

Settled in 1776, Niagara-on-the-Lake was the first capital of Upper Canada. The town was occupied and burned in the War of 1812, as was nearby Fort George.

Destroyed by American gunships during the war, Fort George has been reconstructed, complete with its impressive ramparts, officers' quarters, barracks, kitchen, artificer's shop and visitors' center.

Every summer Niagara-on-the-Lake hosts the internationally acclaimed Shaw Festival, which each year attracts hundreds of thousands of theatre-goers. Ten plays by George Bernard Shaw or his contemporaries are produced annually and presented at the Court House Theatre, the Royal George Theatre and the Festival Theatre.

Above and right: Various views of Niagara-on-the-Lake.

Below: The Niagara River Recreation Trail runs 56 kilometres from Niagara-on-the-Lake to Fort Erie. This scenic, paved trail is ideal for cycling, jogging or for a leisurely walk.

With exhibits and historic reenactments, Fort Erie recreates
the life of an 18th-century soldier.

Below: Fort Erie Race Track is one of the most beautiful
thoroughbred racetracks in North America.

FORT ERIE

Historic Fort Erie sits where the Niagara River
meets Lake Erie. The fort was built by the British in
1764 and captured by Americans during the
War of 1812. After American troops departed it fell into
disrepair until its restoration in 1939.

From May to September Fort Erie is open to visitors. Tours
are led by guides dressed in the uniform of the Glengar-
ry Light Infantry and other period dress. With its draw-
bridge, bastions and dry ditches, the fort is a military en-
thusiast's dream. A museum and period rooms recreate
the harsh life of a 19th-century soldier, as well as colony
men, women and children. In August, Living History
Weekend reenacts the Siege of Fort Erie and full-dress
military drills.

Fort Erie is the southern terminus of the Niagara River
Recreation Trail, an 8-foot-wide paved path that runs 35
miles along the river, from Fort George on Lake Ontario
down to Fort Erie. Historic markers along the way edu-
cate the hikers and cyclists who enjoy this scenic byway.